CPA Exam Review

AT
LEAST
KNOW
THIS

Auditing
and Attestation

1. Introduction and Professional Responsibilities

	Audit	Attestation	Review and Compilation
During engagement with nonpublic company, accountant is subject to:	Clarified Statements on Auditing Standards (SASs) issued by	Statements on Standards for Attestation Engagements (SSAEs) issued by	Statements on Standards for Accounting and Review Services (SSARSs) issued by
	AICPA Auditing Standards Board.	AICPA Auditing Standards Board.	AICPA Accounting and Review Services Committee.

- All statements are recorded in the AICPA Professional Standards. SAS sections have identifier AU-C. SSAE sections have identifier AT-C. SSARS sections have identifier AR-C.

Attestation Audit, review or agreed-upon procedures engagement to report about whether a subject matter or assertion is in conformity with selected criteria.

Audit Form of attestation in which practitioner obtains reasonable assurance that subject matter is in conformity with applicable financial reporting framework, where subject matter is a historical financial statement(s).
- Objective is to determine if financial statements (FS) are presented fairly.
- Determination is based on auditor obtaining reasonable assurance that FS are free from material misstatement, whether due to fraud or error.
  - **Reasonable assurance** High level of assurance, but not absolute.
  - **Materiality** Total misstatement large enough to influence economic decisions of users on the basis of FS.

Auditor responsibility
- Auditor always has general responsibility to conduct audit in accordance with **Generally Accepted Auditing Standards**. GAAS are made of the above Clarified Statements on Auditing Standards and recorded in AICPA Professional Standards.

Client responsibilities
- To prepare and fairly present FS in accordance with the applicable financial reporting framework.
- To maintain internal controls for FS preparation.
- To provide the auditor with:
  - All information, of which management is aware, that is relevant to FS preparation.
  - Other information at request of auditor.
  - Unrestricted access to personnel to obtain audit evidence.

Audit for public company Sarbanes-Oxley Act (SOX) of 2002 established the Public Company Accounting Oversight Board (PCAOB). To conduct an audit of a public company, SOX requires auditor to register with the PCAOB.

During audit with public company, accountant is subject to:	Auditing Standards (AS) issued by
	PCAOB with the approval of SEC.

General standards
- Adequate technical training, proficiency.
- Independence.
- Due professional care.

Standards of fieldwork
- Adequate planning and supervision.
- Sufficient evidence to give reasonable basis for conclusion.
- Adequate understanding of internal control (IC).

Standards of reporting
• Report states engagement, responsibility assumed by practitioner, and opinion/lack of opinion.
• Report states whether or not in accord with GAAP.
• Report states any inconsistent application of GAAP.
• Report states any inadequate disclosure.

PROFESSIONAL RESPONSIBILITIES

This section deals with the AICPA Code of Professional Conduct, Part 1 — Members in Public Practice. This would only bind members of AICPA, except that many states hold that it also binds those doing the work of CPA.

Threat Relationship or condition that could impair a member's compliance with the code.
- **Self-review** Member prepares source document for attest client, without client accepting management responsibility.
- **Self-interest (adverse-interest)** Member does not act with objectivity because interests are aligned with (opposed to) client.
- **Advocacy** Member loses sight of objectivity, becomes client advocate instead.
- **Undue influence** Member defers to client because of client's reputation or dominant personality.
- **Familiarity** Member becomes too sympathetic or accepting of client as a result of close relationship.
- **Management participation** Member takes on management responsibilities.

Conceptual framework When the code is silent, follow this general framework to determine whether you should perform the service or not.

1. Identify and evaluate threats to compliance with code.

Threat(s) is not significant:	Threat(s) is significant:
You may perform service.	Go to 2.

2. Identify and evaluate safeguards.

Risk of noncompliance is at acceptable level:	Risk of noncompliance is not at acceptable level:
You may perform service.	Do not perform service.

Independence Independence conveys neutrality and fairness to management and to users of the financial statements.

Definitions
- **Covered member** One of the following:
  - Individual on attest engagement team.
  - Individual positioned to influence attest engagement team.
  - Partner who provides more than 10 hours of nonattest service to attest client.
  - Partner in same office as lead partner on attest engagement team.
  - CPA firm and firm's benefit plan.
  - Company whose policies are controlled by a covered member
- **Immediate family** Spouse and dependents.

Independence precludes relationships that appear to impair a member's objectivity.
- Member firm is not independent of attest client when:
  - Member firm performs nonattest service for attest client and is found to assume management responsibility.
    - To preserve member's independence, client should (1) assume management responsibility (2) maintain internal controls (3) oversee service. And member firm should establish in writing with client that client accepts management responsibility.
  - Covered member or immediate family has:
    - Direct financial interest in client, material or immaterial (e.g. covered member owns one share or covered member is general partner in partnership that owns one share).
    - Indirect financial interest in client, material only.
  - Covered member or immediate family has a loan to or from (1) client (2) client officer or director (3) individual holding 10% or more of client equity.
  - Covered member or immediate family has a joint closely held investment with client that is material to covered member.
  - Any partner or professional employee, combined with immediate family, has more than five percent of client ownership interests.
  - Any partner or professional employee is simultaneously associated with client as employee, etc. during engagement. Immediate family are permitted to work as employees, but not in a key position (one that prepares or influences FS or components).

- Member cannot accept a contingent fee for performing attest engagement, tax return or claim for tax refund.
  - Member may accept a contingent fee for representing the client in court.
- Member cannot accept commission for recommending a client if member performed attest engagement for client.
  - Member may accept commission for recommending a client if member performed nonattest engagement for client and member discloses commission to client.
- The independence tests for accepting gifts and entertainment are subjective. Gift from client is allowed as long as it is "clearly insignificant to the member" (for perspective, the test used to be $100), and entertainment is allowed as long as it is "reasonable in the circumstances."

- For public companies, the PCAOB holds that CPA firm is not independent of attest client when:
  - Firm provides any of the following: bookkeeping services, valuation services, HR services, investment services, or legal services.
  - Firm plans or counsels aggressive or confidential tax position.
  - Firm provides tax service to person in FAR oversight role. **Exception** New hires with fewer than 180 days on job, board members, and affiliates.
  - Firm receives contingent fee or commission.

Engagement that requires independence	Engagement that does not require independence
• Audit. • Review. • Agreed-upon procedures. • Compilation report that does not disclose lack of independence. ✓ • Examination of Prospective Financial Statements i.e. financial forecast.	• Tax. • Consulting. • Preparation of Financial Statements. • Compilation report that discloses lack of independence. ✓

• Audit, review and agreed-upon procedures are all attestation engagements. Attestations require independence. • Compilation is not an attestation according to SSAE, but it is according to SSARS. Compilations do not require independence, but those without independence must at least disclose.

Documents compiled during audit

Working papers prepared by members.	Do not need to provide to client.
Work product prepared by member.	May withhold from client for the following reasons: • Payment is outstanding. • Work product is unfinished. • Compliance with ET. • Ongoing litigation with client.
Documents provided by client.	Must return to client at client's request.

• **Confidential Client Information Rule** Member should not disclose any confidential client information without consent of client. Includes the act of taking copies of confidential info after member leaves CPA firm—even if only for educational purposes. Excludes subpoena, AICPA or state board inspection, peer review.

Quality Control (QC) Objective is to provide reasonable assurance at the firm level that professional services conform with auditing and accounting standards. **Note: Do not confuse quality control of CPA firm with internal control of the client.**

QC Elements
- Leadership understands QC and recognizes its imperative.
- Firm sets policies for reasonable assurance that personnel comply with ethical/independence requirements, confirmed in writing.
- Firm accepts only those clients the firm can serve competently and ethically.
- Firm hires only those personnel that can perform competently and ethically.
- Firm sets policies for reasonable assurance that engagements are reviewed, and disagreements between members are documented.
- Firm monitors QC for reasonable assurance that QC system is effective and communicates results annually.
- Firm documents QC system.

QC Monitoring Activities

CPA firm without public clients	CPA firm with public clients

• Peer review by AICPA once every three years.
• Peer review is conducted by state CPA society or AICPA National Peer Review Committee.
• There are two types of peer review:
  o System review includes test of recent engagements and test of firm's system of QC.
  o Engagement review includes test of recent engagements only.
	• Inspection by PCAOB once every year (for firm with 100+ audit reports of public companies) or once every three years (for firm with 100 reports or fewer).
	• Inspection is conducted by PCAOB employee.
	• Inspection always includes test of recent engagements and test of firm's system of QC.

2. Basic Concepts, Fraud and Planning

BASIC CONCEPTS

Audit steps
1. Plan audit.
2. Obtain understanding of company and its environment.
   - Risk assessment procedures
   - Test of controls
3. Assess risk of material misstatement and design further audit procedures.
4. Run further audit procedures and evaluate evidence obtained.
   - Test of controls
   - Substantive procedures
     - Test of details
     - Analytical procedures
5. Report on financial statements.

Financial statement assertions Claims by management that are explicit or implicit in the FS. Classified as follows so that auditor knows to test.

- ✔**Existence, occurrence** ex. Inventory exists; Sale occurs.
- ✔**Rights, obligations** ex. Company owns or constructively owns fixed asset; Disclose contingency according to GAAP.
- ✔**Completeness, cutoff** ex. All AP is reported; Sale is in the correct accounting period.
- ✔**Accuracy, valuation** ex. AR is correct in amount.
- ✔**Classification, understandability** ex. Obligation is in correct account i.e. long term because of intent and ability to refinance; Cost is expensed, rather than capitalized, when appropriate.

- Most important assertions for AR: existence and valuation. For AR, overstatement is a serious risk. • Most important assertions for AP: completeness. For AP, understatement is a serious risk. The way to prove completeness is to look at invoices paid after year end, and check the dates of those invoices.

Audit risk The risk that the auditor gives reasonable assurance when, in fact, FS contain material misstatements.
- Audit risk = Inherent risk * Control risk * Detection risk

Inherent risk (IR) Risk of a misstatement in an assertion which is material to FS, without regard to company's internal control.	Control risk (CR) Risk that company's internal control will not prevent misstatement, or detect and correct on a timely basis.	Detection risk (DR) Risk that the auditor fails to detect misstatements.
Dependent on client and client environment.	Dependent on client internal controls.	Dependent on the nature, timing and extent of further audit procedures.
ex. Company has higher inherent risk if officers receive bonuses based on reported income.	ex. See Chapter 3.	ex. See Chapter 4.
Risk of material misstatement (RMM) Inherent risk and control risk are collectively called the risk of material misstatement. RMM is assessed by risk assessment procedures. We say RMM is independent of the audit because RMM is revealed through testing, not altered by the amount of testing.		Unlike RMM, the auditor can decrease DR solely by doing more testing. If RMM is assessed high, then the acceptable DR is lower and the auditor is required to obtain more persuasive audit evidence to lower DR. This can be accomplished by changing the nature, timing and extent of further audit procedures.

- Mathematics of audit risk is secondary. Just know that the acceptable DR has an inverse relationship to RMM.

DR is the risk that the auditor fails to detect mest.
  - the auditor can decrease DR
    by DOING MORE TESTING

If RMM is assessed HIGH — then DR o/b lower
(it can be lowered
by obtaining more
persuasive evidence).

Materiality Auditor has responsibility to consider the concept of materiality in determining risk assessment procedures, assessing RMM, determining further audit procedures, and assessing the outcome.

Materiality for FS as a whole	Performance materiality
Total misstatement large enough to influence economic decisions of users on the basis of FS.	Performance materiality is a lesser amount to decrease risk that the aggregate of misstatements exceed materiality for FS as a whole.

● Materiality may be revised at any time. ● Materiality and performance materiality also exist at assertion level. ● **Tolerable misstatement** Performance materiality in sampling. See Chapter 7.

Using the work of a specialist Specialist may be related to client, though it is not preferable. Note: Internal auditor is not a specialist.
- Specialist understands and agrees to a supporting role in the audit.
- Auditor evaluates work for adequacy, including source data, significant assumptions and methods, and conclusion.
- Auditor should not refer to specialist in report with unmodified opinion.
  - Reference to specialist in opinion does not change auditor's responsibility for opinion.

FRAUD

Fraud An intentional and deceptive act that results in a misstatement of FS. Act may be committed by individual(s) from within company or from without.
- If fraud is identified or suspected, it's incumbent on auditor to decrease DR to acceptable level.
- DR is highest for **fraud committed by upper management**, since upper management has the power to override controls and alter accounting records. DR is less for **fraud committed by lower management**, and least for **errors** because there's no concealment associated with errors.
- Auditor adopts an attitude of professional skepticism: Auditor presumes there is RMM in revenue recognition and management override of controls. Auditor does not presume that management is either honest or dishonest.

Auditor responsibility
- Auditor is responsible for obtaining reasonable assurance of detecting misstatements, due to fraud or error.
- Auditor is not responsible for detecting fraud (primary responsibility belongs to management and those charged with governance).
- Auditor is not responsible for planning an audit to discover financial stress of employees or adverse relationship between company and employees (assess only if it comes to his or her attention).

Fraud types
- **Fraudulent financial reporting** Fraud by the company. ex. Inventory overstatement.
- **Misappropriation of assets** Fraud on the company. ex. Defalcation; Employee theft.

Risk factors

Fraudulent financial reporting	Misappropriation of assets
- Fast rate of change in industry. - High growth and profitability within industry. - High turnover of accounting personnel. - Negative cash flows from operations. - Overly complex structure, unusual lines of authority. - Management by one or a few individuals. - Management compensation in form of bonuses. - Management presses to meet or exceed forecasts. - Management promotes aggressive reporting. - Non-financial management concern for accounting principles.	- Large amounts of cash processed. - Small, expensive inventory items.

● The following conditions are usually present in instances of fraud: incentive/pressure, opportunity, and rationalization/attitude. ● The following are not risk factors: Insiders purchased additional stock in company; Significant outstanding checks at year-end; Computer-generated documents; Year-end adjusting entries.

Fraud steps

1. Assess RMM due to fraud.	<ul><li>Inquire of management: how they internally assess RMM due to fraud, what is their assessment, do they have knowledge of actual or suspected fraud.</li><li>Inquire of internal auditor: what is their assessment of RMM due to fraud.</li><li>Inquire of those charged with governance: how do they oversee management, do they have knowledge of actual or suspected fraud.</li><li>Use analytical procedures to identify unusual relationships, especially for revenue accounts.</li></ul>	
2. Obtain appropriate audit evidence based on assessment.	For assessed RMM due to fraud	For assessed risk of management override of controls
	<ul><li>Use less predictable, unannounced audit procedures.</li><li>Supervise engagement team more closely.</li><li>Emphasize subjective over objective transactions.</li><li>Conduct test counts at year end, all on one date, rather than more analytical procedures.</li></ul>	<ul><li>Assess appropriateness of journal entries made to general ledger, adjustments and those made directly to financial statements.</li><li>Review accounting estimates for bias.</li><li>Evaluate business rationale for big transactions.</li></ul>
3. Respond appropriately to identified or suspected fraud.	Auditor has discretion	Auditor has obligation
	<ul><li>Auditor may withdraw from engagement at his or her discretion in the following cases:<ul><li>Company does not take appropriate action.</li><li>Risk of fraud is high and pervasive.</li><li>Management competence or integrity is doubtful.</li></ul></li></ul>	<ul><li>Auditor communicates with management no matter how small the fraud. If fraud within management, communicate with those charged with governance (i.e. board of directors).</li><li>Auditor keeps client information confidential, except to the following parties:<ul><li>To SEC on reporting an auditor change, due to fraud, on Form 8-K.</li><li>To government agency that funds company.</li><li>To successor auditor who makes inquiries.</li><li>In response to subpoena.</li></ul></li></ul>

- List of events that constitute a reportable event is beyond the scope of this exam.

NONCOMPLIANCE WITH LAWS AND REGULATIONS

Auditor responsibility	No responsibility
<ul><li>For noncompliance which has direct material effect on FS, auditor is responsible for obtaining reasonable assurance of detecting misstatements.</li><li>For noncompliance which may have indirect material effect on FS, auditor is responsible for the following limited audit procedures:<ul><li>Inquire of management and those charged with government.</li><li>Inspect correspondence with regulatory agencies.</li></ul></li></ul>	<ul><li>Auditor is not responsible for preventing or detecting noncompliance (the primary responsibility belongs to management and those charged with governance).</li></ul>

3. Respond appropriately to identified or suspected noncompliance.	<ul><li>If company does not take appropriate action, auditor may place less reliance on management representations, and may withdraw from engagement.</li><li>According to Private Securities Litigation Reform Act of 1995, if company does not take appropriate action and refuses to inform SEC, auditor reports to SEC directly, within one business day.</li></ul>

AUDIT PLANNING

Preconditions for acceptance
- Auditor determines that FS reporting framework is acceptable.
- Management accepts their responsibilities, see Chapter 1.
- Management does not limit scope of engagement.

Communicate with predecessor **prior to** acceptance of engagement Auditor asks client to authorize the predecessor to respond to inquiries.
- Auditor is required to discuss the following with predecessor:
  - Information as to integrity of management.
  - Disagreements with management about accounting/auditing.
  - Reason for the change in auditor.
- In the event that client refuses to allow inquiries, or in the event that predecessor has highly negative opinion, the auditor should consider the implications. Auditor is not required to withdraw.

Written engagement letter

Auditor must include	Auditor may include	Auditor must exclude
<ul><li>Audit objective, audit scope, reporting framework.</li><li>Auditor responsibilities:<ul><li>Conduct according to GAAS.</li><li>Understand IC.</li><li>Communicate IC significant deficiencies and material weaknesses to management.</li></ul></li><li>Management responsibilities.</li><li>Inherent limitations of audit and internal controls, i.e. the risk of material misstatements passing undetected.</li></ul>	<ul><li>Timing of audit in general for client assistance.</li><li>Predecessor auditor.</li><li>Additional services provided.</li><li>Opportunities to improve operations or controls.</li><li>Fees.</li></ul>	<ul><li>Timing of audit fieldwork.</li><li>Auditor responsibility to <u>search for</u> IC significant deficiencies.</li></ul>

- Timing of inventory count will be coordinated with management because it requires client assistance.

Written overall audit strategy

Written audit plan

Written overall audit strategy	Written audit plan
<ul><li>Identify the characteristics of the engagement that affect its scope (e.g. industry reporting requirements, regulatory audit requirements, number and location of components to audit, usability of the work of internal auditors, usability of audit evidence from previous audits).</li><li>Identify company's reporting objectives, including reporting timetable.</li><li>Consider other factors, including materiality and high risk areas.</li><li>Consider the results of **preliminary engagement activities**.</li><li>Plan how to deploy resources (e.g. number of team members and number or hours) and whether or not to involve specialists for complex matters.</li></ul>	<ul><li>Describe the nature and extent of planned risk assessment procedures.</li><li>Describe the nature, timing and extent of planned further audit procedures at the relevant assertion level.</li><li>Describe other planned audit procedures.</li></ul>

- **Preliminary engagement activities** Auditor evaluates its own quality control, and agrees to terms in engagement letter. <u>For continuing clients</u>, auditor can always begin this part of the audit at interim date.

3. Risk Assessment Procedures

Auditor obtains an understanding of the company and its environment, including the IC, with the objective of assessing RMM. **Risk assessment procedures** are procedures which enhance this understanding.
- Inquiry of management.
- Analytical procedures.
- Observation and inspection.
- Review of prior year working papers and permanent file.
  - The following are not risk assessment procedures:
    - Inquiry of legal counsel.
    - Substantive tests.
    - Confirmation and reevaluation.

New client
- **Communicate with predecessor <u>after</u> acceptance of engagement** It is customary for auditor to review predecessor working papers on audit planning (NOT the predecessor engagement letter), IC, audit results and analysis of balance sheet accounts and contingencies. If this review indicates that prior year FS may require revisions, then auditor arranges to meet with client and predecessor.

Continuing client
- Review prior year working papers and permanent file for client.

Analytical procedures Study of relationships within financial and nonfinancial data. <u>Analytical procedures are required during risk assessm</u>ent.
- Form an expectation about relationships, and compare expected relationship to actual.
- Here are some of the relationships to examine:
  - Current year data compared to prior year data (AKA Horizontal analysis).
  - Current year data compared to budget for current year.
  - Account balances as a percentage of other account balances (AKA Vertical analysis).
    - ex. Current ratio; Gross margin percentage.
  - All of the above compared to industry data.
- Use analytical procedures to identify inconsistent or unexpected relationships and to plan additional audit work.

	AP	Inventory	AR
Turnover	Purchases / average AP	COGS / average inventory	Sales / average AR
Conversion period	Average AP / (purchases / 365)	Average inventory / (COGS / 365)	Average AR / (sales / 365)
Days outstanding	Ending AP / (purchases / 365)	Ending inventory / (COGS / 365)	Ending AR / (sales / 365)

- Alternatively, turnover is calculated using ending AP/inventory/AR in denominator. • When turnover is greater than 1, turnover <u>decreases</u> when numerator and denominator increase by same amount (e.g. end of year sale causes AR turnover to decrease).

Using the work of internal auditors
Auditor may use the work of internal auditors as long as auditor assesses competence and objectivity. This way, the evidence gathered by the internal auditor affects the nature, timing and extent of the auditor's procedures. But external auditor retains sole responsibility for audit opinion and risk assessments therein. And auditor should not use work of internal auditor when there is a lot of judgment involved and when there is a high RMM.

UNDERSTAND INTERNAL CONTROL

Auditor obtains an **understanding of the internal controls relevant to the audit**. Understanding IC is part of understanding the company, so the objective is the same: to assess RMM.

Understanding of the internal controls...	<ul><li>Includes design and implementation of controls.<ul><li>Walkthrough tests design effectiveness of controls. For public companies, walkthrough is required for each major class of transaction. Consists of tracing a transaction from start to inclusion in FS, talking to employees at each step in the process: What is your understanding of your task? Do you perform on timely basis? What do you do when you find an error? What errors have you found? Have you been asked to override the control?</li></ul></li><li>Excludes operating effectiveness of controls, which is addressed by test of controls.</li></ul>
...relevant to the audit	Includes controls the company uses for achievement of (1) reporting objectives. Company uses controls for other purposes—for achievement of (2) operations and (3) compliance objectives—but these controls are only relevant in the context of what is reported.

Components of internal control CRIME

Control environment	Management forms a culture of honesty and ethical behavior. This is the foundation for the other components. For public companies, SEC requires audit committee composed of 3-6 members independent members—in this context, independence just means that committee member is not part of day-to-day management—and at least one financial expert. Audit committee (1) appoints, compensates external auditors, (2) oversees internal audit, and (3) oversees anonymous fraud hotline. Control environment is bolstered by strong audit committee.
Risk assessment process	Company has its own process to identify RMM. Inappropriate or ad hoc process could represent a significant deficiency or material weakness.
The information system	Company starts and records transactions. Company pays special attention to how information is transferred to general ledger, how significant accounting estimates are recorded, and how nonstandard journal entries are recorded.
Control activities	<ul><li>Performance reviews</li><li>Information processing</li><li>**Physical controls** Restrict access to blank time cards, blank checks, etc.</li><li>**Segregation of duties** Segregate authorization, recording, and custody.</li></ul>
Monitoring of controls	Company has its own process to monitor controls. Includes reviews of internal audit department, and analysis of operating reports to identify control failures. ex. Report comparing budgeted income statement to actual income statement.

- There are inherent limitations to internal control. Most common examples include risk of human error, risk of management override, risk of employee collusion, and the constraint that cost of IC should not exceed benefit. This means that, at best, company has only reasonable assurance of achievement of control objectives.

Documentation of understanding of internal control

Auditor documents using either questionnaire, narrative/memoranda, or flowchart. In practice, most auditors use questionnaires. Questionnaires are the least time-consuming, and they've already been proofed and peer-reviewed (if packaged with auditing software), whereas you auditor be relying on auditor's own understanding if he or she creates narrative or flowchart.

ASSESS INTERNAL CONTROL

For audit of public company, auditor must perform test of controls—auditor must also issue report on the effectiveness of IC (see Chapter 5). For audit of nonpublic company, auditor performs test of controls if either of the following is true:

- CR is expected to be less than maximum and test of controls is cost effective.
- Without test of controls, substantive procedures don't provide sufficient evidence.

Auditor performs test of controls	Auditor does not perform test of controls.
Assuming test of controls shows IC to be operating effectively, auditor assesses RMM as low. This means acceptable DR is higher, and auditor has luxury of planning fewer substantive procedures, using internal evidence, performing interim tests, lowering sample size.	Assuming auditor does not perform test of controls—or test of controls shows IC to be operating ineffectively—auditor assesses RMM as high. This means acceptable DR is lower, and auditor has to plan greater substantive procedures, using direct external evidence, performing tests at year-end, raising sample size.

- Substantive procedures may not provide sufficient evidence in all cases. To a greater extent, companies use technology for both operations and financial reporting. Where audit evidence is only available in electronic form, quality of the evidence depends on internal control.
- **Cost effective** Auditor predicts that test of controls combined with fewer substantive procedures is more cost effective than no test of controls and greater substantive procedures.
- RMM must be assessed at BOTH the financial statement level and the assertion level.
- Auditor is permitted to assess RMM at the same time as obtaining an understanding of the company.

Test of control methods
- (1) Inquiry
- (2) Observation
- (3) **Document examination** Involves searching for signatures, dates and checklists. For example, auditor notes date of bank reconciliation to see how soon it was performed.
- (4) **Reperformance** Auditor does his or her own calculations and compares to what client has.

Directional testing
- Existence testing
  - Auditor may test any account for existence, but AR and Inventory draw a lot of existence testing because of the **risk of overstatement**, which is the risk that reported population is larger than true population.
  - Auditor starts with General Ledger (reported population) because it's potentially larger, then searches backwards for the source document.
  - ex. If auditor can't "vouch" sales account to sales invoice, AR may be overstated.
- Completeness testing
  - Auditor may test any account for completeness, but AP draws a lot of completeness testing because of the **risk of understatement**, which is the risk that true population is larger than reported population.
  - Auditor starts with source documents (true population) because they're potentially larger, then searches for inclusion in General Ledger.
  - ex. If auditor can't "trace forward" receiving report to entry in journal, AP may be understated.

Revenue and collection controls
- Sales department…
  - …to check inventory availability.
  - …to create sales order.
  - …to send copy of sales order to shipping department, pending credit approval.
- Credit department…
  - …reports to treasurer
    - …to check credit.
- Warehouse…
  - …to pick inventory based on ticket generated by sales order.
  - …to send goods and ticket to the shipping department.
- Shipping department…
  - …to compare physical count of inventory, ticket, and sales order.
  - …to create bill of lading, which the carrier signs to verify the goods are shipped.
  - …to send copy of bill of lading to accounting department.
  - …to take delivery of returns of merchandise.
- Accounting department AKA AR, Billing...
  - …reports to controller
    - …to create sales invoice.
    - …to send copy of sales invoice to customer.
    - …to debit AR and credit revenue account.
- Mailroom…
  - …to create check listing (AKA cash receipts listing, remittance listing)—two employees should open the mail.
  - …to send checks and check listing to cashier.
  - …to send copy of check listing to accounting department.

- Cashier…
  - …reports to treasurer
    - …to deposit to bank.
- Accounting department
  - …reports to treasurer
    - …to debit cash and credit AR.
- Treasurer…
  - …to approve write-offs.

- Bank accounts should be reconciled by someone independent of cash custody and recordkeeping.
- Prenumbering (e.g. sales orders, receiving reports, etc.) generally supports completeness because you can trace forward one source document at a time.
- Periodic count to adjust inventory supports assertions of valuation, existence.
- In a reconciliation of AR control total and AR subsidiary ledger (AKA AR listing of customer balances), the subsidiary balance is the one that governs because AR without a customer is not an AR. This is another important aspect of internal control: periodic reconciliation will lower RMM.
- Bank lockbox is alternative way to receive cash which prevents employees from diverting checks.
- For a small business, accounting department approves credit memos for lack of another option, and business owner should review.

Revenue and collection test of controls
- Observation: Observe consistency of employee's use of cash registers.
- Observation: Observe employee prepare schedule of past due AR.
- Document examination: Examine sales revenue entries for evidence of shipping documents.
- Document examination: Examine sales invoices for evidence of credit checks—this supports valuation assertion for AR NRV.
- Document examination: Examine date that credit is applied to AR balance for customer C as compared to date of bank deposit from customer C. **Lapping** Accountant steals portion of customer A's deposit, applies customer B deposit to customer A balance, applies customer C deposit to customer B balance, etc. In this case, credit won't be applied to balance for customer C until company receives money from customer D—long after the deposit cleared from customer C.

Acquisition and expenditure controls
- User group/store…
  - …to create the requisition (purchases department does not create/authorize, nor does it receive the bids from suppliers).
- Purchases department…
  - …to pick supplier and negotiate price.
  - …to create PO.
  - …to send "blind" copy of PO to receiving (i.e. copy shows all info except quantity).
- Receiving department…
  - …to make independent count of goods received.
  - …to create receiving report.
  - …to send copy of receiving report to AP department.
- Accounting department AKA AP…
  - …reports to controller
    - …to agree vendor invoice to receiving report to PO.
    - …to create **voucher**—shows accounts that are debited and credited.
    - …to debit inventory or expense account and credit cash or AP account.
    - …to send voucher package to disbursements.
- Disbursements…
  - …reports to treasurer
    - …to create check.
    - …to sign and mail check (treasurer does not send back to AP for mailing).
    - …to stamp voucher "Paid" to prevent duplicate payment.

- Employee with check-signing authority should not have edit access to accounting records.
- Company should receive several bids when purchase exceeds certain amount. Cost is not the only consideration in choosing a bid.
- Generally, AP is recorded when client receives goods.

Acquisition and expenditure test of controls
- Observation: Observe receiving department make the count.
- Document examination: Examine the date of receipt of goods as compared to the date recorded in voucher package.
- Document examination: Examine invoice for initials of employee who matched invoice to receiving report to PO.
- Document examination: Examine paid vouchers for "Paid" stamps.
- Document examination: Examine cancelled checks for authorized signatures.

Personnel and payroll controls
- Human resources…
  - …to approve pay rate, changes in pay rate.
  - …to approve deductions.
  - …to send notice of employee termination to payroll department.
- Payroll department…
  - …reports to treasurer
    - …to distribute paychecks.
    - …to deposit unclaimed payroll into special bank account.

- Employee should sign for payment if payment is made in form of cash.
- Time tickets support valuation of costs (i.e. costs are assigned to direct labor or overhead, as appropriate).

Personnel and payroll test of controls
- Inquiry: Inquire about segregation of payroll authorization and paycheck disbursement.
- Reperformance: Multiply number of hours by wage rate and compare to paychecks.

Financing controls
- Board of directors…
  - …to authorize issues of debt and equity.
- Stock registrar…
  - …independent of company
    - …to verify that issues have been properly authorized.
- Stock transfer agent…
  - …independent of company
    - …to keep stockholder records.
    - …to make transfers of stock ownership.

- Cancelled stock certificates should be defaced to stop reissue.

Financing test of controls
- Document examination: Read minutes from board of directors meeting for evidence of authorization of stock options and dividends.

Investing / Property, Plant and Equipment controls
- Board of directors…
  - …to authorize purchases of PPE over certain amount.
- Treasurer…
  - …to take custody of marketable securities, stored in a bank safe-deposit box, along with one other employee.

- Internal auditor (or other employee who does not have authorization, recording or custody) should do periodic inspections of securities and PPE to compare to subsidiary ledger.
- Ideally, company will use independent stockbroker, bank or trust company to take custody of marketable securities; Treasurer is next best option.

Internal control deficiencies
Auditor is not required to search for deficiencies in internal control for neither public nor nonpublic companies. But auditor should evaluate the severity of those deficiencies that come to his or her attention.

- **Deficiency** Control does not allow company to prevent, or detect and correct, misstatements on a timely basis.
- **Significant deficiency** Deficiency which is less severe than than material weakness.
- **Material weakness** Deficiency which creates reasonable possibility of a material misstatement on FS.

Auditor of nonpublic company communicates, in writing, to management and governance:	Auditor of public company communicates, in writing, to management and governance:
<ul><li>Significant deficiencies</li><li>Material weaknesses</li></ul>	<ul><li>Deficiencies</li><li>Significant deficiencies</li><li>Material weaknesses</li></ul>

● Deficiencies may be partially offset by compensating controls, but not eliminated. ● For prior year deficiencies that company has not corrected, auditor is required to re-communicate. ● Auditor should not write in the communication, "No significant deficiencies were found" because audit is not designed to detect significant deficiencies.

Auditor has 60 days after release date of auditor's report to send IC communication. Auditor may send early communication for company to take corrective action. As long as auditor has time to run new tests of IC, auditor is allowed to issue unmodified opinion on IC over financial reporting.

4. Substantive Procedures

Auditor obtains sufficient, appropriate audit evidence to respond to the assessed risks of material misstatement at the financial statement level.

Appropriateness Quality of evidence, including relevance and reliability.
- Relevance is how testing relates to the purpose of your testing. For example, when the objective is to test AP for understatement, it is not relevant to test the recorded AP.
- Reliability of evidence is greater:
  - When evidence is obtained from outside the company.
  - When there is effective IC.
  - For original documents rather than for photocopies.
  - For observation rather than for inquiry.

Substantive procedures Objective is to detect material misstatements in FS. Substantive procedures include:
1. **Test of details** Test of transactions and test of financial balances. Classic example of test of details is AR confirmation.
2. **Analytical procedures** Study of relationships within financial and nonfinancial data. If auditor finds inconsistent or unexpected relationship in the course of doing analytical procedures, he or she should perform test of details.
   - Analytical procedures are optional during substantive procedures, whereas they are required during risk assessment (see Chapter 2) and final review.
   - Analytical procedures are effective for:
     - Income statement accounts, since they are more predictable than balance sheet accounts.
     - Rent revenue ex. Estimate using rental rates, average number of units and average number of vacancies, then compare for reasonableness.
     - Interest expense ex. Estimate using balance of bonds payable, then compare for reasonableness.
     - Payroll expense ex. Estimate using tax rates, then compare for reasonableness.
       - Accounts with a lot of data/transactions.

Accounting estimates Objective is to determine whether FS accounting estimates are reasonable.
- Accounting estimates are susceptible to management bias, and biased estimates increase the risk of material misstatement.
- Instead of regarding accounting estimates one at a time, auditor should consider management bias by looking at all accounting estimates for the year, and how those estimates compare across several years of FS.
- Risk assessment procedure for accounting estimates:
  - Obtain understanding of management's process of making accounting estimates, and how management responds to new events that create or affect estimates. Make inquiries of management.

Audit documentation AKA Workpapers, Working Papers Objective is to keep a record of procedures and evidence that form the basis for auditor's report.
- Auditor is required to document:
  - Overall audit strategy, including changes to strategy.
  - Audit plan, including changes to plan.
- Extent of documentation: Enough for experienced auditor to understand—one with no previous connection to the audit.
  - Factors that affect documentation:
    - RMM, especially CR.
    - Size and complexity of company.
    - Type of audit procedures and audit evidence.

Current File	Permanent file
• **Lead schedule** A summary of the components of an account. ex. Cash lead schedule is a summary of the cash accounts, includes cross-references to supporting documents like bank confirmations and bank reconciliations. • **Working trial balance** Spreadsheet with columns for unaudited trial balance, adjustments and reclassification.	• Organizing documents of corporation. • Continuing contracts (e.g. leases, bonds). • Minutes from stockholder meetings. • Schedule of equity accounts. • PY FS, audit reports.

- After document completion date, auditor should not delete or discard audit documentation for a minimum of 5 years. For public companies, retention period is 7 years.

TEST OF DETAILS

Cash
- AICPA publishes a standard bank confirmation form which prompts bank for balances of all cash accounts—and balances of all liability accounts with associated collateral.
- **Schedule of interbank transfers** List prepared by auditor to detect kiting. Shows bank transfers at end of year, date recorded in cash disbursements journal, date recorded in cash receipts journal.
- Auditor uses proof of cash when there is weak internal control.

Accounts receivable
- Auditor may test any account for existence, but AR draws a lot of existence testing because of the risk of overstatement.
- Auditor is required to use external confirmation procedures unless one of the following is present:
  - Overall balance is immaterial.
  - Confirmation procedures would be ineffective.
  - RMM is low.
- **Positive Confirmation** Request for customer to reply directly to auditor to confirm or reject AR balance. Positive confirmations produce reliable audit evidence, support existence assertion. Despite this, risks include: (1) source is not authentic (2) source is not knowledgeable (3) information is compromised.
  - When response is by fax or email, auditor requests original paper copy or calls to validate identity.
  - When auditor worries customer is signing without paying attention to balance, auditor uses "blank" confirmation.
  - When customer isn't able to confirm account balance, auditor requests for customer to confirm or reject individual invoice.
  - Nonresponse:
    - Ask client to reach out to customer.
    - Alternative procedures provide less reliability: Use cutoff bank statement to prove AR was received the following year; use shipping documents to prove company shipped merchandise before year-end.
- **Negative Confirmation** Request for customer to reply directly to auditor only if customer disagrees with AR balance. Negative confirmations are less persuasive as audit evidence.
  - Generally, auditor does not use negative confirmations unless all of the following is present:
    - AR consists of small individual balances.
    - RMM is low.
    - Low exception rate is predicted.
    - No condition exists that would cause requests to be disregarded.

Inventory
- Auditor tests existence and condition (i.e. valuation) of inventory.
  - Auditor attends physical inventory counting to:
    - Observe management's count (existence).
    - Perform test count (existence).
    - Inspect inventory (valuation).
  - Auditor does analytical procedures like inventory turnover, see Chapter 2, to support valuation.

Property, plant and equipment
- Auditor tests account to detect overstatement in account.
  - Auditor tests PPE to detect overstatement of PPE, i.e. repairs and maintenance was mislabelled as PPE.
  - Auditor tests repairs and maintenance to detect overstatement of repairs and maintenance, i.e. PPE was mislabelled as repairs and maintenance.
- Auditor vouches PPE additions and retirements during the current year. Generally, auditor does not test prior year PPE.

Accounts payable
- Auditor reviews all cash payments for a sufficient time—one month is not a sufficient time—after the Balance Sheet date to verify there are no unrecorded liabilities.
- Trace receiving reports and vendor invoices to AP ledger to verify there are no unrecorded liabilities.
  - Auditor may test any account for completeness, but AP draws a lot of completeness testing because of the risk of understatement.

Confirmation is a reliable substantive procedure, the auditor's first choice of procedures for the following accounts:
- Cash account — confirmation by bank.
- Accounts receivable — confirmation by customer.
- Investments are — confirmation by brokerage, independent custodian.
- Loans, collateral — confirmation by bank, recent lender.
- Bonds payable — confirmation by bondholder, bond trustee.
  - For bonds payable, reading the bond indenture is a reliable alternative procedure.
- Stock outstanding — confirmation by independent registrar, transfer agent.

OTHER AUDIT EVIDENCE

Client representation letter AKA Written representation Objective is to obtain written statement from management expressing that they have fulfilled the responsibilities of engagement letter, including fair presentation of FS and completeness of information to auditor.
- Letter is required, but it does not affect, let alone replace, the nature and extent of audit evidence.
- Letter includes representation that management has made available or disclosed to auditors:
    - Minutes from meetings of those charged with governance.
    - RMM due to fraud.
    - Related party transactions.
    - Communications from regulators about noncompliance or deficiency of financial reporting.
    - Known or possible litigation, claims and assessments.
    - Subsequent events that require adjustment to FS.
- Letter is signed by both Chief Executive Officer and Chief Financial Officer.
- Letter is dated on same date as auditor's report.
- When letter is not furnished—always treated as scope limitation—or letter is unreliable, auditor generally issues a disclaimer of opinion. The reason is that auditor is unable to obtain sufficient appropriate audit evidence, and the effects on the FS are pervasive.
- When auditor has concerns about integrity of management, withdrawal is an option.

Litigation, claims and assessments (LCA) The main procedures for identifying LCA are:
- Make inquiry of management about policies for identifying, evaluating and accounting for LCA.
- Obtain from management a description and evaluation of LCA.
- Obtain written representation from management (i.e. client representation letter) that all known or possible LCA were disclosed to auditor.
- Review minutes from meetings of those charged with governance; review invoices from legal counsel; review correspondence between company and legal counsel.

Letter to legal counsel Objective is to corroborate information about LCA provided by management.
- Letter contains a list prepared by management of all LCA. Ask legal counsel if it agrees with this list, including nature of the matter, likelihood of unfavorable outcome, estimate of loss. Ask legal counsel if letter contains a complete list of LCA.
- When there's a scope limitation, auditor generally issues a disclaimer of opinion.

Scope limitations	No scope limitation
<ul><li>Legal counsel refuses to furnish information requested.</li><li>Legal counsel is not able to estimate the likelihood of unfavorable outcome or amount of potential loss.</li></ul>	<ul><li>Legal counsel limits response to matters to which they have given substantive attention.</li><li>Legal counsel limits response to material matters only.</li></ul>

Subsequent event Event occurring after date of FS and before date of auditor's report.

Condition existed at BS date.	Condition did not exist at BS date.	Condition did not exist at BS date, but omission will make report unreliable.
Recognize	Do not report	Disclose
ex. Bad debt expense; Warranty expense; Legal settlement if event pre-existed.	ex. Sale of bond or CS; Loss of assets from fire; Foreign currency loss; Legal settlement if event did not pre-exist.	ex. Significant merger or legal settlement if event did not pre-exist, such that omission would make financial statements "misleading."

Objective is to identify subsequent events which require recognition (i.e. adjustment) or disclosure in the FS. The main procedures for identifying subsequent events are:
- Make inquiry of management about policies for identifying subsequent events.
- Make inquiry of management about whether subsequent events have occurred or not.
- Read minutes from meetings of those charged with governance.
- Read interim financial statements.

Subsequently discovered fact Fact that becomes known to auditor after date of auditor's report.
- Auditor has no responsibility to identify subsequently discovered facts. For subsequently discovered fact that becomes known to auditor:
    - Auditor discusses with management and considers revision to FS.
    - When auditor requests revision BUT management refuses, auditor should modify the opinion.

Omitted procedures discovered after date of auditor's report
- Auditor has no responsibility to review audit work after report release date. For omitted procedure that becomes known to auditor:
    - If auditor believes (1) omission affects present ability to support audit opinion and (2) users likely to rely on audit report, auditor does omitted procedure, or alternative procedure, to support audit opinion.
    - If auditor is unable to perform omitted procedure, auditor goes to legal counsel for advice.

5. Reporting

Audit with unmodified opinion for nonpublic company

Title	Independent Auditor's Report
Addressee	Auditor's client, usually the auditee but sometimes a third party.
Introductory	We have audited FS of X Company, which comprise the balance sheet as of Dec. 31, 20X1 and 20X0, and the related statements of income, changes in stockholders' equity and cash flows for the years then ended, and the related notes.
Management responsibility	Management is responsible for fair presentation of FS according to GAAP, including maintenance of IC.
Auditor responsibility	Our responsibility is to express an opinion on FS. We conducted audit according to GAAS. We must obtain reasonable assurance that FS are free from material misstatement. An audit involves procedures to obtain audit evidence about the amounts and disclosures in FS. We assess RMM, whether due to fraud or error. We assess IC over preparation of FS in order to choose appropriate audit procedures, not to express opinion on IC. We also evaluate appropriateness of accounting policies used, reasonableness of accounting estimates by management, and overall presentation of FS. We believe we have sufficient and appropriate audit evidence to make opinion.
Opinion	In our opinion, FS present fairly, in all material respects, *[position, operations and cash flow]* according to GAAP.
Signature block	Auditor signature; auditor city and state; date

Audit with unmodified opinion for public company

Title	Report of Independent Registered Public Accounting Firm
Addressee	To the shareholders and the board of directors of X Company
Opinion	We have audited the balance sheets of X Company as of Dec. 31, 20X1 and 20X0, the related statements of income, comprehensive income, changes in stockholders' equity, and cash flows for each of the three years in the period ended Dec. 31, 20X1, and the related notes. In our opinion, FS present fairly, in all material respects, *[position, operations and cash flow]* according to GAAP.
Basis for opinion	These FS are the responsibility of management. Our responsibility is to express an opinion on FS based on our audits. We are a public accounting firm registered with the PCAOB and are required to be independent in accordance with securities laws and regulations of SEC and PCAOB. We conducted audits in accordance with PCAOB standards. Those standards require that we plan and perform the audit to obtain reasonable assurance about whether FS are free of material misstatement, whether due to error or fraud. Our audits included performing procedures to assess RMM, whether due to error or fraud, and performing procedures that respond to those risks. Such procedures included examining, on a test basis, evidence regarding the amounts and disclosures in FS. Our audits also included evaluating the accounting principles used and significant estimates made by management, as well as evaluating the overall presentation of FS. We believe that our audits provide a reasonable basis for our opinion.
Critical audit matters (if applicable)	The critical audit matters (CAM) below are matters arising from the current period audit of FS that were communicated or required to be communicated to the audit committee and: (1) relate to accounts or disclosures that are material to FS and (2) involved our especially challenging, subjective, or complex judgments. The communication of CAM does not alter in any way our opinion on FS, taken as a whole, and we are not, by communicating CAM, providing separate opinions on these matters or on the related accounts or disclosures. *[Include critical audit matters]*
Audit of internal control	We have also audited, in accordance with standards of PCAOB, the effectiveness of [name of auditee] internal control over financial reporting as of [FS date], based on criteria in Internal Control—Integrated Framework by COSO of the Treadway Commission and our report dated [date of audit report on internal control] expressed an unqualified opinion thereon.
Signature block	Auditor signature; auditor tenure; auditor city and state; date

● This report assumes auditor issues a separate report on IC over financial reporting. Public company has to issue a report on FS as well as a report on IC over financial reporting. Auditor may issue one integrated report or separate reports, as seen here. ● **Auditor tenure** "We've served as X's auditor since [year]." ● **Date** Date that auditor obtains sufficient appropriate evidence, not before FS is prepared nor before client representation letter is submitted.

AUDIT REPORTS WITH UNMODIFIED OPINIONS

Going concern uncertainty—Unmodified opinion—Additional emphasis-of-matter ¶ about going concern uncertainty.
- Objective is to conclude whether there is substantial doubt about company's ability to continue as going concern for a reasonable period of time, where reasonable period is less than 1 year.
- Audit procedures in regular course of audit are usually sufficient, including:
  - Analytical procedures.
  - Review of subsequent events.
  - Review of compliance with debt agreements.
  - Confirmation with third parties about continued financial support.
- Auditor considers mitigating events before reaching conclusion. Mitigating events include:
  - Plans to decrease expenses.
  - Plans to dispose of assets.
  - Plans to borrow or restructure.
  - Plans to increase owner's equity.
- When auditor concludes there is substantial doubt, company makes adequate disclosure and auditor adds emphasis-of-matter paragraph.
  - Extra paragraph contains the terms "Substantial doubt" and "Going concern."
  - If company does not make adequate disclosure, auditor treats like a GAAP departure, below.
- When auditor finds no more cause for doubt in subsequent year, auditor does not add emphasis-of-matter paragraph—even if company presents comparative FS.

Inconsistency in application of GAAP—Unmodified opinion—Additional emphasis-of-matter ¶ about inconsistency.
- When auditor concludes that a change in accounting principle has a material effect on comparability of FS (one period to another), auditor adds emphasis-of-matter paragraph to unmodified report.
  - ex. Change of inventory method; Change of construction method.
- For a change in accounting principle to be reported this way, it meets all of the following criteria:
  - New principle complies with accounting framework.
  - Accounting for change in principle complies with accounting framework.
  - Disclosures for change in principle are adequate.
  - Company justifies that new principle is preferable.
- If it does not meet these criteria, auditor treats like a GAAP departure, below.
- When change in accounting principle will have a material effect on comparability of FS—but not until a future year—auditor does not add emphasis-of-matter paragraph until that future year.

Group financial statements
- Group auditor takes full responsibility for work of component auditors—**Unmodified opinion**.
- Group auditor does not take full responsibility for work of component auditors—**Unmodified opinion**—Changes to auditor responsibility and opinion ¶.
  - Additional language: "...We did not audit the FS of Co., a wholly-owned subsidiary, which reflect total assets constituting % of consolidated total assets and total revenues constituting % of consolidated total revenues. Those FS were audited by other auditors whose report has been furnished to us, and our opinion, insofar as it relates to the amounts included for subsidiary, is based solely on the report of the other auditors."
- In all situations, group auditor obtains understanding of component auditor's independence and professional competence, reads the component auditor's report for significant findings, and communicates with component auditor when necessary.

AUDIT REPORT WITH MODIFIED OPINION

All of the following are considered modified opinions:
- **Qualified opinion** Except for one or more issues, FS present [position, operations and cash flow] in accordance with GAAP.
- **Adverse opinion** FS do not present [position, operations and cash flow] in accordance with GAAP.
- **Disclaimer of opinion** No opinion on fairness of FS.

GAAP departure
- ex. Company doesn't report illegal act; Company does not disclose going concern uncertainty on FS; Company makes unjustified change in accounting principle.
- GAAP departure does not have pervasive effects on FS—**Qualified opinion**—Change to opinion ¶ and additional basis for opinion ¶.
  - Revision to opinion ¶ of qualified opinion: "In our opinion, except for the <u>effects of</u> the matter described in the Basis for Qualified Opinion paragraph, the FS present fairly…"
- GAAP departure has pervasive effects on FS—**Adverse opinion**—Change to opinion ¶ and additional basis for opinion ¶.
  - Pervasive effects on FS include:
    - Effects that are not confined to specific accounts.
    - Effects that make up a substantial portion of FS.
    - Effects that are fundamental to user's understanding of FS.
  - If departure is immaterial, auditor issues **unmodified opinion**.
  - **Accounting principles rule** Departure from GAAP or other applicable financial reporting framework is permitted if it would be misleading to use framework (e.g. new legislation, new type of business transaction). Auditor describes the departure and why it would be misleading.

Scope limitation Restriction on auditor such that auditor is unable to obtain sufficient appropriate evidence.
- Scope limitation does not have pervasive effects on FS—**Qualified opinion**—Change to opinion ¶ and additional basis for opinion ¶.
  - Revision to opinion ¶ of qualified opinion: "In our opinion, except for the <u>possible effects of</u> the matter described in the Basis for Qualified Opinion paragraph, the FS present fairly…"
- Scope limitation has pervasive effects on FS—**Disclaimer of opinion**—Changes to introductory ¶, auditor responsibility ¶, opinion ¶ and additional basis for opinion ¶.
  - If scope limitation is immaterial or if auditor does alternative procedure, auditor issues **unmodified opinion**.

- **Client-imposed scope limitation** Client restricts auditor access to information.
  - ex. Client refuses to allow auditor to make inventory count or send confirmations.
  - One consequence is that auditor doubts management integrity, so withdrawal is an option.
  - Note: This is not the same as a limited reporting objective. Sometimes, auditor is hired to report on just one financial statement. No scope limitation exists as long as auditor has access to all information.
- **Circumstance-imposed limitation** Circumstances restrict auditor access to information.
  - ex. Accounting records were destroyed; Auditor was hired too late to perform all substantive procedures.
  - Auditor is allowed to give split opinions on component financial statements, but not on component accounts.
    - ex. Auditor is not hired in time to observe beginning inventory, so he or she disclaims opinion on income statement. As long as auditor observes ending inventory, he or she is still allowed to issue unmodified opinion on balance sheet.

AUDIT OF INTERNAL CONTROL

Public companies have two additional requirements, according to SOX Section 404.
1. Management needs to do <u>assessment</u> of internal control over financial reporting.
2. Auditor needs to do <u>audit</u> of internal control over financial reporting AKA audit of internal control. PCAOB's Auditing Standard 5 is authoritative for auditor who does the audit of internal control.

1. Management assessment should contain:
- Statement of management's responsibility for internal control.
- Framework used to assess internal control.
    - The most common framework is <u>Internal Control</u> — <u>Integrated Framework</u> by the Committee of Sponsoring Organizations (COSO).
- Assessment of the effectiveness of internal control over financial reporting.

2. **Audit of internal control** Objective is to express opinion on the effectiveness of internal control over financial reporting. To express an unmodified opinion, auditor obtains reasonable assurance that material weaknesses do not exist as of the end of the company's fiscal year. Auditor uses the same date and framework for the audit as management does in their own assessment.
- See Chapter 3 for definition of material weakness. The following are indicators of material weakness:
    - Auditor detects fraud by senior management.
    - Auditor detects material misstatement.
    - Company issues restatement to correct material misstatement.
    - Audit committee lacks effective oversight.
- Auditor may provide unqualified opinion for material weakness that is detected and corrected before the end of the company's fiscal year.

Top-down approach to audit of internal control
- Auditor determines area of testing by identifying significant accounts or disclosures.
    - **Significant account or disclosure** One with reasonable possibility that it contains a material misstatement.
    - Auditor uses a walkthrough, see Chapter 3, for significant accounts to allow auditor to gain sufficient understanding of the control.
- Emphasis on entity-level controls. There is benefit to effective entity-level controls, which is that auditor may decrease testing on process-level controls.

Opinions for audit of internal control

Unqualified opinion	Adverse opinion	Disclaimer of opinion
Auditor obtains reasonable assurance that material weaknesses do not exist.	One or more material weaknesses exist. ex. Ineffective oversight of financial reporting by the audit committee.	Auditor cannot perform all procedures which are necessary to form opinion.

- For the audit of internal control, unlike the main audit, there is no opinion between unqualified and adverse.

Critical audit matters (CAM)
- Audit should identify each current-year CAM; describe why it was identified as CAM and how it was addressed; and mention the related financial statement accounts or disclosures.
- Audit with unmodified opinion or qualified opinion may include communication of CAMs.
- Audit with adverse opinion or disclaimer of opinion should not include communication of CAMs since the most important matter to discuss is the reason for these opinions.

6. Compilation and Review

SSARS issues standards for:

	Preparation of Financial Statements	Compilation	Review
Accountant prerequisites	• Compliance with ET, professional judgment, knowledge of accounting system in company and accounting framework in industry.	• Compliance with ET, professional judgment, knowledge of accounting system in company and accounting framework in industry.	• Compliance with ET, professional judgment, knowledge of accounting system in company and accounting framework in industry. • Independence.
Objective	• Prepare FS pursuant to accounting framework.	• Assist management in preparing FS without obtaining assurance. Issue report, but disclaim assurance.	• Obtain limited (negative) assurance that accountant is not aware of any material misstatements in FS.
Procedures	• Prepare FS using accounting framework, describe framework in notes to FS.	• Read FS for format, obvious material misstatement. • Inform management of incorrect information, request management to correct. • Propose revisions for inadequate description of framework, known departures from framework, misleading elements. ○ Do not make inquiries or review information from company. ○ Do not modify report to state "FS is not in conformity with GAAP" because this is viewed as expressing an opinion.	• Read FS, interim financial information, subsidiary FS, minutes from owner meetings, director meetings. • Run analytical procedures: Compare forecast to actual; Study ratios of FS elements for plausibility. • Reconcile FS to interim FS. • Make inquiries of management: FS conforms to GAAP? Significant transactions near end of period? Subsequent events? Fraud suspected? • Communicate with management on all significant matters, inconsistent relationships, unusual or complex situations, subsequent events. • If FS could be materially misstated, accountant performs additional procedures. • Request written representation letter stating management has fulfilled responsibilities of engagement letter, above all to fairly present FS. ○ Do not send bank confirmation letters, perform cutoff tests, or test internal control. ○ Do not modify report to state "FS is not in conformity with GAAP" because that's expressing an opinion.
Report	• There isn't generally a report—but if disclaimer is not on each page of FS, then accountant will disclaim in one-sentence report.	• For standard report, see SSARS 21, Section 80, .A43, Illustration 1. • **Title** Accountant's Compilation Report • **Date** Date that accountant completes compilation procedures. ○ No compilation report is necessary if written engagement letter bans third-party use and all pages of FS carry disclaimer "Restricted for management use only."	• For standard report, see SSARS 21, Section 90, .A147, Illustration 2. • **Title** Independent Accountant's Review Report • **Date** Not before accountant obtains limited assurance based on his procedures, and management takes responsibility for FS.

Modifications to report	• There are no modifications to report.	• Non-GAAP framework which is not described in FS. • Known departure—if readily apparent—and effects of departure. • Client omits substantially all disclosures. Use this: "Omitted disclosures might influence user's conclusions, FS is not designed for users who don't know of disclosures." • Accountant is not independent.	• Non-GAAP framework which is not described in FS. • Known departure and effects of departure. • Client omits substantially all disclosures. Use this: "Omitted disclosures might influence user's conclusions, FS is not designed for users who don't know of disclosures." • Any matter that the accountant thinks is fundamental to users understanding of FS—even if it's already disclosed in FS. • For reviews that are meant for specified parties only, include this in extra paragraph ("Review should not be used by anyone other than specified parties").
Recourse to withdraw	• Client omits substantially all disclosures and there's an intention to mislead.	• Accountant is unable to complete engagement because management failed to provide records. • Modification to report is not enough to relate all deficiencies in FS. • Client omits substantially all disclosures and there's an intention to mislead. • Client does not revise nor disclose in FS, and accountant elects not to disclose departures.	• Accountant is unable to complete some aspect of procedures. • Modification to report is not enough to relate all deficiencies in FS. • Accountant doubts management's integrity such that it still doesn't find written representations reliable. • Accountant thinks there is material misstatements due to fraud or due to noncompliance with laws and regulations. • Accountant is not independent.

• Link for standard reports: http://www.journalofaccountancy.com/content/dam/jofa/archive/issues/2014/12/ssars-21-final.pdf • In all cases, client signs a written engagement letter, accepting responsibility for framework, internal control, fraud, informing accountant. For compilation and review, client also accepts responsibility for fair presentation of FS. • Do not modify report solely for inconsistent application of GAAP or doubt about ability to stay going-concern. Neither of these are treated as departures from GAAP **unless** they are not adequately disclosed in FS. At that point, accountant should modify report the same way as in a departure. • If client asks to change from audit to review, accountant can issue review report instead as long as there is reasonable justification for the change. Do not mention original engagement in review report. • SAS not SSARS is applicable to interim review of client for which you or predecessor performed audit. • PCAOB not SSARS is applicable to interim review of publicly traded company.

7. Audit Sampling

Audit sampling Auditor's use of less than 100% of the data to make a conclusion about the whole data set.

Statistical sampling Procedure in which auditor uses laws of probability to measure the risk. Even a randomly selected sample is not statistical without statistical evaluation of the risk and results.
- Sample size is the same for a statistical sample as it is for a nonstatistical sample.

Sampling risk The risk that the auditor makes the wrong conclusion because the sample does not represent the entire population.
- Sampling risk = 1.00 - Confidence level (AKA Reliance level)

Types of sampling risk
- Sampling risk that affects audit effectiveness, i.e. audit never reaches correct opinion.
  - Risk of assessing control risk too low (AKA over reliance): Risk that control in population is <u>less effective</u> than in sampling.
  - Risk of incorrect acceptance: Risk that recorded amount in population has <u>greater misstatements</u> than in sampling.
- Sampling risk that affects audit efficiency, i.e. audit eventually reaches correct opinion, but needs additional testing to get there.
  - Risk of assessing control risk too high (AKA under reliance): Risk that control in population is <u>more effective</u> than in sampling.
  - Risk of incorrect rejection: Risk that recorded amount in population has <u>fewer misstatements</u> than in sampling.

Planning for sampling tests
- The primary variable in sampling is the acceptable level of sampling risk. Auditor can't choose the sample size until this is set. The auditor decides for him or herself whether 1% sampling risk (99% confidence) is needed, or 2% sampling risk is acceptable instead. There's a whole set of data tables for 1% sampling risk, and another set for 2%.

TYPES OF SAMPLING PLANS

Attributes sampling Tests the rate of occurrence in a sample to make conclusion about rate in population. Used in test of controls to test rate of deviation (i.e. rate of departure from expected performance of control).
- The word "rate" is a giveaway that you're dealing with attributes sampling, not variables sampling.

Approaches for attributes sampling:
- **Fixed sampling** Single step plan.
- **Sequential sampling** (AKA stop-or-go testing) Multiple step plan with one step affecting the next.
- **Discovery sampling** Appropriate when expected deviation rate is zero or near zero.

Make selection	• It is not appropriate to test only high dollar items in test of controls. All items in population should have equal chance of getting selected. <u>Simple random and systematic random</u> are the only statistical methods of selecting a sample.
	  ○ In simple random, auditor matches random numbers with numbered documents.
	  ○ In systematic random, auditor starts with random unit, then selects every nth unit (so there's no need for numbered documents). Interval is found by dividing population by sample size. One danger of this method is that interval may coincide with unknown pattern in population.

	• Block selection is the least representative form of selecting a sample.

Choose the size	• Acceptable sampling risk is inverse to sample size.
	  ○ For attributes sampling, this is the risk of overreliance because consequences of over reliance are more serious than consequences of underreliance.
	• Tolerable rate of deviation in population is inverse to sample size.
	  ○ Tolerable rate of deviation is the maximum rate auditor will allow without altering assessed level of control risk. Auditor will let the tolerable rate be high if assessed control risk is high, or if the control is not significant to audit.
	  ○ Since not all deviations in control result in misstatements, tolerable rate is higher for controls than for test of details.
	• Expected rate of deviation in population is proportional to sample size.

Test	• Deviation includes:
	  ○ Item is not properly approved.
	  ○ Item is not located, despite alternative procedures.
	• Deviation excludes:
	  ○ Voided item.
	  ○ Unused item (e.g. skipped check).
	  ○ Inapplicable item (e.g. utility bill doesn't have PO).

	• When auditor discovers voided/unused/inapplicable item, auditor documents and adds replacement item to sample.

Evaluate the results	• Find sample deviation rate, which is the number of observed deviations / sample size.
	 • Given acceptable sampling risk and sample deviation rate, use a table or computer program to look up the upper deviation limit (i.e. maximum deviation) in the population.
	   ○ Upper deviation limit = Sample deviation rate + Allowance for sampling risk
	   ○ You may be asked to solve one variable given the other two, but not to mathematically derive either the upper deviation limit or the allowance for sampling risk. That's beyond the scope of the exam.
	 • If upper deviation limit is less than tolerable rate of deviation, sample supports original assessment of control risk. If not, auditor either increases assessment of control risk or does additional control testing that, hopefully, supports original assessment.

Variables sampling Tests the dollar amount in a sample to make conclusion about dollar amount in population. Used in test of details.

Approaches for variables sampling

Monetary Unit Sampling (MUS) Dollar has equal chance of selection, and dollar pulls entire transaction into sample. Transaction does not have equal chance of selection.	**Classical Variables Sampling** Transaction has equal chance of selection.
• Sample size is not based on standard deviation because PPS selects dollars and each dollar in the population is the same size. • Appropriate when objective is to detect overstatement, as in tests of AR. • Not appropriate to detect understatement, because smaller dollar items have less chance of selection. Zero and negative dollar items have no chance.	• This technique is based on normal distribution theory. For example, auditor determines sample size by estimating standard deviation in a preliminary sample. • Appropriate when objective is to detect understatement, as in tests of AP. Test does not need to be specially altered for items with small or negative balances. • Normal distribution theory is not appropriate for (1) large items or differences between items, and (2) sample size is small. • More complex than MUS such that auditor generally needs computer program to design.

	Monetary Unit Sampling	**Classical Variables Sampling**
Make selection	• MUS is a subset of probability proportional to size (PPS) sampling.	• **Stratification** Act of dividing population into groups with similar characteristics. Objective is to decrease the variance/standard deviation, and thereby decrease the sample size. • In practice, auditor stratifies the population of sales invoices so unusually large invoices will be pulled in for audit.
Choose the size	• Acceptable sampling risk is inverse to sample size. ○ For variables sampling, this is the risk of incorrect acceptance because consequences of incorrect acceptance are more serious than consequences of incorrect rejection. • Tolerable misstatement in population is inverse to sample size. • Expected misstatement in population is proportional to sample size. • Assessed level of control risk is proportional to sample size. • Variance within population is proportional to sample size—applies to classical variables sampling only.	
Test ✳	**Recorded value less than sampling interval** Recorded value: $500 Audited value: $496 Sampling interval: $1,000 • Projected misstatement = 4 * 1,000 = $4,000 ✳ ✳ **Recorded value greater than sampling interval** Recorded value: $500 Audited value: $496 Sampling interval: $400 • Projected misstatement = $4 ✳ (whatever the difference is)	Population: 5,000 items Total recorded value in population: $500,000 Average recorded value in sample: $99 Average audited value in sample: $95 **Mean per unit** • ETAV = 5,000 * 95 = $475,000 • Projected misstatement = $25,000 • Allowance for sampling risk is based on variance of audited amounts in sample. **Ratio estimation** • ETAV = 500,000 * (95 / 99) = $479,798 • Projected misstatement = $20,202 • Allowance for sampling risk is based on variance of recorded-audited differences. **Difference estimation** • Projected misstatement = (99 - 95) * 5,000 = $20,000 • Allowance for sampling risk is based on variance of recorded-audited differences.

Evaluate the results	• Request management to record adjustments for the factual misstatements identified in the sample.
	• Withdraw the factual misstatements that are corrected by management. Do not adjust the projected misstatements.
	• Compare the tolerable misstatement to the upper limit of misstatement (total adjusted factual and projected misstatement + allowance for sampling risk). Generally, if tolerable misstatement is less than the upper limit, sample results support the conclusion that account is not materially misstated.

• **ETAV** Estimated Total Audited Value. • Size of population has virtually no effect on size of sample, unless population is very small. • Ratio estimation and difference estimation are more efficient than mean per unit because they manage with smaller sample sizes. But neither technique is appropriate when there are insufficient differences in the sample: the result is a zero allowance for sampling risk, which is impossible in audit sampling.

8. Technology

General controls Company-wide policies for access rights and systems change management.
Application controls Input, processing and output controls of an application.

EFFECT OF TECHNOLOGY ON INTERNAL CONTROL

For all of the ways technology supports efficiency, security and decision-making, it also increases the complexity of internal controls and the difficulty in managing risks. Here are some of the specific risks cited by the Committee of Sponsoring Organizations (COSO):
- Management lacks understanding of the applications that affect financial information.
  - Control: Walkthrough of IT function.
- Risk of misstatement due to errors in end-user computing.
  - Control: Make use of IT-supported applications.
- Use of spreadsheets for closing journal entries like LIFO and FV adjustments to PPE.
  - Input control: Reconcile source documentation to input.
  - Access control: Access is limited, secured with password.
- Technology is outsourced to third party.
  - Control: Review controls at the third party or obtain SSAE report on controls.
- Security parameters like password length/complexity is not applied consistently.
  - Control: Establish a system for rating the importance of the application to the financial reporting process.

Additional controls:
  - Audit trail detects unauthorized access to the system; allows company to reconstruct the steps that led to breaches and system failures; monitors user activity.
    - Batch transaction processing creates better audit trails than online transaction processing.
  - Digital certificate confirms that the message received was not tampered during transmittal.

COSO differentiates between centralized and distributed data processing.
- **Centralized data processing** Processing done by one or more large computers at one site.
- **Distributed data processing** Processing done by end user computers.

Distributed data processing

Benefits
- Affordability.   - Backup flexibility.
Risks
- Inefficient use of resources.   - Potential for deletion of audit trail.   - No segregation of technology functions.
- These risks can be mitigated by establishing a corporate IT function, a standard setting body, and central testing for software.

AICPA notes that, in some cases, technology makes it impossible for auditor to obtain evidence via substantive procedures. When company conducts business using IT and doesn't produce documentation of transactions, auditor has to use tests of controls to obtain sufficient, appropriate audit evidence.

TEST OF CONTROLS

For the auditor to rely on application controls, he or she uses computer-assisted audit tools. Note: Auditor is not required to perform test of controls for nonpublic company, see Chapter 2, but it means that control risk is assessed at the maximum.

Tests of design effectiveness Auditor uses tests of design effectiveness to gain understanding of application logic; to identify unauthorized changes in application's source code; and to verify the copy of current version of application. Computer expertise is required.
- Code review
- Flowcharting software
- Snapshot

Tests of operating effectiveness

Test data Auditor runs its own valid and invalid transactions through a copy of current version of application that it obtains from client IT. Auditor compares test results to expected results. ex. Does application prevent transactions with invalid POs, transactions above the credit limit?	**Integrated data check** Auditor runs its own valid and invalid transaction through module designed into the application. Auditor compares test results to expected results. ITF is tested during normal business operations without the operator's knowledge.	**Parallel simulation** Auditor runs actual client transactions through auditor's generalized audit software, or a replica of the application created by the auditor. Auditor compares test results to client's results.
Benefits		
• Computer expertise is not required.	• Client's IT is not involved.	• Client's IT is not involved. • Test results are compared to client's results, not expectations.
Risks		
• Client's IT provides current version. • Tested at one point in time. • Test is inefficient.	• Potential to corrupt client file.	• Replica is not exact.

We are a young business with a lot to prove.

The best way to help us is by submitting

your feedback to admin@atleastknowthis.com.

Made in the USA
Middletown, DE
02 August 2019